Dedication

My story is lovingly dedicated to anyone feeling heartbroken,

heavy burdened and alone. I pray that God folds you into his

loving embrace and brings sweet healing to your soul.

You are Not Alone

Kari Jobe

You're my strength

You're my defender

You're my refuge in the storm

Through these trials

You've always been faithful

You bring healing to my soul

I am not alone

I am not alone

You will go before me

You will never leave me

Introduction

There are many, many mothers and fathers who are experiencing similar tragedies as me, so what makes me so special? Absolutely nothing. I don't claim to be a Bible scholar, or an expert on grieving; heck, I'm still learning as I go. And I'm definitely not a professional author. In fact, this is the first book I have ever tried to write. All I know is that God put a burning desire in my heart to share my story in the hopes of helping someone, anyone, who is struggling with grief and doubting, or questioning their faith. If I help even one person by writing this, then I have accomplished my goal.

I just want you to know in your heart, and with every fiber of your being that God WILL NOT and HAS NOT left you. He is there, all you have to do is call out to Him.

Matthew 11:28

Then Jesus said ,"Come to me, all who are weary and heavy burdened, and I will give you rest."

YET WILL I TRUST HIM

August 30th, 2016 started off like any other day. It was hot and
muggy, as always in South Carolina in August, as I went to work
at my brand new job as an Optometry Technician in a small office
on the other side of town. Little did I know that my whole world
would be turned upside down that very afternoon. I had just
gotten home from work and was reading a cheesy romance novel
on my Kindle after having dinner, when I got the call that every
parent prays to never get. It was the call telling me that my 24 year
old son had passed away. I don't even remember the
conversation. I just remember dropping the phone and not being
able to catch my breath. I must have hyperventilated or fainted
because the next thing I remember is waking up on my husband's
old recliner with my family anxiously leaning over me.

My baby was gone, just like that. For one brief, crazy second I
remembered thinking that if i just hadn't answered the phone ,

that he would still be alive. Crazy, right? It's as if I had instantly lost my grip on reality.

My sweet, bashful son who had the funniest laugh and loved to cook, had lain face down on his apartment floor all alone for 3 days before his body was discovered by his landlord. This is an image that will absolutely haunt me for the rest of my life.

After 6 months of investigation, and several phone calls to the coroner, it was ruled that Kevin had died from a Carfentanil overdose. There was a small bag of white powder that tested positive for Carfentanil in his apartment, but no drugs found in his body. But, because it takes such a small amount to stop a person's heart, they believe that there wasn't enough of the drug in his system for them to trace. They deemed it to be an accidental overdose, but in my heart, I knew the real truth. I believe my son had given up on life.

Looking back Kevin was a happy, well adjusted kid with the most beautiful brown eyes and long dark eyelashes. He had perfect skin that tanned beautifully in the summer. We were all so jealous of that skin! In his younger years, you would never see him without his stuffed Tweety Bird under his arm. That poor thing had been drug through the mud so many times that I was constantly having to stitch the eyes back on it. Whenever Tweety got a bath in the washing machine, Kevin would be right there waiting for it. As he got older, he always talked of becoming a famous chef and would spend hours cooking up amazing meals! He loved looking up complicated recipes and challenging himself to try to make them. One of my favorites was his steak with garlic marinade, it literally would melt in your mouth. He truly was a natural in the kitchen, but the mess he made was epic! There wouldn't be an inch of clean countertop space when he was finished, and I thought I would go broke buying all of those crazy ingredients, but it was totally worth it. It made him happy, and we were always more than willing to be his taste testers! He also had a small lawn mowing business in our neighborhood by the time he was only 12 years old. He had the keys to several of our neighbors' sheds, and kept a dry erase board on his wall with his mowing schedule on it, as well as all of his customer's phone numbers. To this day I still think of him every time I see a dry erase board. He truly was one of the most responsible and organized people that I have ever known. He tried to teach me his organizational skills too, but soon gave up after realizing I was just a hopeless cause. Not only was Kevin a super responsible kid, but he also was very sweet natured, affectionate, and loved giving hugs and making homemade gifts for me. I still have a concrete stepping stone that he made for me that has his name and handprint in the middle of it. He spent days making that for me, and I will forever cherish it. One particularly sweet memory I have of his childhood, is on Thursday nights me and my two boys would watch American Idol together on my bed. We refused to miss a show because we had made it our special little tradition. The bed would be completely covered in snacks, blankets, and pillows, and we would always argue the whole time about who the best singer was, and sometimes the boys even ended up in a wrestling match over it! Oh how I miss those precious times, and what I would give to just turn back the clock. Kevin was always so ambitious too, I'll never forget the day he was accepted into the early college program at his high school. He was so excited and had this huge, goofy smile on his face when he told me the good news. We even danced a jig across the living room floor to celebrate! I was so happy for him. He had big plans for his life, and I had no doubt that he would accomplish every one of them.

Over the next couple of years I started seeing a gradual change in Kevin's personality though. My once happy, affectionate, and motivated son was growing distant and at times frighteningly angry. I went from being his confidant and superhero to his #1 arch enemy. He went from laughing and playing with his little brother, to resenting him and ignoring him. He became very sullen and began to get dark circles under his eyes. I have never felt so helpless in all of my life, I didn't know what was wrong with him. I went into his room every night before bed and prayed with him and I begged him to open up to me, but he refused to confide in me or to a counselor. He would verbally lash out at me, his brother, and my husband (Kevin's step-father), and I am ashamed to say that I often became impatient and frustrated with him. This went on for a few years and by the time he came of age the tension in our house had become unbearable. He decided to move out and I was truly worried that our relationship was forever ruined, and also very concerned for his safety. But surprisingly, and much to my relief, we actually talked quite often after he moved out , so I'm pretty sure that he missed me as much as I missed him.

Eventually Kevin fell on some rough times financially and moved back home. That's when I saw first hand just how bad things had gotten, he just seemed so sad and emotionally detached from everything. I finally talked him into seeing a doctor in a nearby city where they eventually diagnosed him with having Major Depression Disorder. They prescribed him various medications which actually seemed to help at the time, but then they would constantly alter the dosages, which would send him on an emotional roller coaster for days, and sometimes weeks on end. 23 years old or not, if I had known then what I know now, I would have stepped in and said "enough!" But when your child becomes an adult, the physicians don't let the parents have much say in the matter. I don't completely blame the doctors though, because I know that by this time Kevin was abusing these medications and manipulating the system to get more.

Desperate to help somehow, I picked Kevin up one weekend and took him to Petco where I decided to adopt a cat for him. It was a young gray female cat that Kevin named Mitten, and boy did he love that cat! He spoiled her completely rotten. He bought her a silver rhinestone collar and treats galore! Whatever that cat wanted, she got. I had hoped that having another life dependant on him would give my son a sense of purpose, and it really seemed to help for quite a long time. He would call me everyday to tell me something funny that Mitten would do, or to ask me for advice on caring for her. I really looked forward to hearing his daily stories about her goofy antics. They were the best of friends.

Everything seemed to be going fairly well after that for a while, until a couple of months later when Kevin had gotten involved in some legal issues and sat me down one day to explain everything. I caught a glimpse of my old Kevin when he said to me "Mom, I really messed up. Can you drive me to the jail so I can turn myself in? I have to fix this." I was so disappointed by his actions, but also proud that he took responsibility for it and was handling it like a man. He ended up with no jail time but with some very hefty fines.

I'm not sure why, but Kevin started to quickly spiral out of control after this happened. He was admitted into the hospital several times in the following weeks because of two near overdoses, and a suicide attempt, and was receiving a lot of intense counseling and therapy. I visited him frequently and attended some counseling sessions with him. It was after one of these particularly difficult sessions where the therapist just couldn't seem to get through to Kevin, that I went out to my car, collapsed in the seat, pounded on the steering wheel, and screamed out to God in fear of my son's life. "Why won't you help him fight this addiction? Why won't you cure him of this horrible depression? Why are you not answering my prayers, where are you!?" And then I pleaded with God to please just let me see my son smile again. It had been so very long since I had seen him truly happy. He always acted so defeated and sad, and I felt powerless to help him, and nothing I did seemed to be helping.

And then a couple of months later, my mom was unexpectedly diagnosed with a terminal, very aggressive form of Uterine cancer. It quickly spread through her body, leaving my brother and I to make the agonizing decision to put her in Hospice care. She was only 67 years old. At one time, my mom and Kevin had a very close relationship, and spent a lot of time together. One of their favorite outings was visiting as many yard sales as they could find on Saturday mornings. Kevin was always super excited to show me all of the treasures he would buy during their shopping sprees. Their close bond caused me to really worry about how my son would handle his grandmas sudden illness and later her passing, but I was very surprised at how unaffected he seemed by it all. Sadly, I think by this point that he was completely numb emotionally, and was just a shell of his former self, and wasn't able to grasp the finality of it all.

Everything with my mom had happened so fast that I don't think she could ever accept the fact that her days were quickly coming to an end. One day when it was just her and I in the hospital room, she turned to me with fear in her eyes and totally broke my heart when she asked me if she was going to die. I didn't want to lie to her, but I didn't want to scare her either. The only thing I could think to say was "I hope not mom." She seemed satisfied with my answer though, and quickly fell back to sleep. My mom passed away just over a week later, and our heads were spinning with shock. She was gone, just like that. To say that I was stressed out and completely emotionally drained would be a huge understatement. There were so many decisions to be made, and so many emotions to deal with in a very short timespan.

It was during this same time that I got a phone call from Kevin telling me that he had been in an altercation with someone and some of his things had been stolen, he wanted me to help him figure out what to do. I was so mentally exhausted that I am ashamed to say that I snapped . I had reached my breaking point (or so I thought), and was incapable of giving any intelligent advise or fixing anything for anybody at that point. "Kevin, I can't do this with you right now, my mom and your grandma, just died! I will have to call you later." He got very angry and hung up on me. It was the only time that I remember him ever doing that, and the only time that we hung up without saying I love you. It was also the last time I ever spoke to my son. I was in another state at this time handling my mom's affairs and had tried to call him back and text him several times, but got no response. I had assumed it was because he was angry with me, but I should have called the police to go check on him. Should've, would've, could've are words that run through my mind constantly, and nearly drive me to the brink of insanity. Knowing that my son was laying there, unable to answer me while I was calling him, absolutely torments me. Dear God, I would give anything to re-do that conversation and go back in time. It plays in my mind like a broken record, and keeps me up at night. How does a person ever forgive themself for something like that? How does a mom live with herself after letting her son down in such a horrible way? Did he harm himself on purpose like he had threatened to do so many times before? I may never know, but I know that he needed me, and I wasn't there for him. A mom is supposed to protect their children, so why do I deserve to go on living when he can't? I literally hated myself and didn't feel I deserved the right to live, or deserved to be loved. I begged God every night to just not let me wake up. I fantasized about sneaking out of my house at night dressed in dark clothing, and walking out in front of traffic.

I had quickly slipped into a very, very dark place emotionally. The guilt and devastation were destroying me physically and mentally. I went from not sleeping or eating at all , to sleeping and eating all the time. Sleeping was the only escape from the pain. At night, I would have terrible nightmares and wake up in a cold sweat. And to this day, I continue to have terrible anxiety attacks. I was so angry at myself, at Kevin, at the people who I felt weren't there for me after he died, and most of all, at God. How could the God of love and compassion take my son and my mom away from me in just 3 months time? They were both too young to die. I didn't even get the chance to say goodbye to my son. I couldn't even see his body or give him one last hug when he passed away. I had been a Christian for nearly 20 years and brought my children up in the church where they were both baptized. We were good people, so why me? Why me Lord?!

I quickly began to completely isolate myself from so many people and push them away. I just couldn't be around anyone, and I definitely couldn't engage in any kind of small talk. Why would I care what color dress someone bought yesterday at the store when my life has just been shattered to pieces? Why would I care what new haircut is in style when I can't even make myself change out of my pajamas? What I needed to talk about was my son. People just didn't understand that I HAD to talk about him in order to keep his memory alive because I'm terrified that everyone will forget him. I could care less about trivial, silly conversation. I just didn't feel like I fit in anywhere anymore, and this caused me to totally isolate myself. It was a very lonely time for me, but all I could concentrate on was surviving minute to minute because I was incapable of thinking or functioning beyond that. Many times I would try to pray for help , but I just couldn't utter a single word. The words just wouldn't come, so I gave up on praying. We have a yellow yard sign in my flower bed next to our driveway that says in big, bold words; "Thank you Jesus" on it. I remember that sign irritating me so much. I felt like it was taunting me every time I got out of my car. I was very tempted to throw it across the yard so many times, but I never had the nerve.

I guess my son Slade grew tired of my catatonic state, because he took me to my favorite park near the beach. We sat on my favorite swing with a perfect view overlooking this lake that has a beautiful fountain in the center, where several swans always congregate. Slade then began to gently tell me just how selfish I was being, and said "I'M still here ya know, and I still need you." And you know what? He was absolutely right. Even though he was 20 years old at the time, he still needed his mom and I needed to be present. He was suffering too, and I needed to be strong for him. He is an amazing son and he deserved that. My husband also deserved to have a wife, not a zombie, and I totally had lost sight of that. What a true blessing those two are to me! This was a real eye opener, and I knew I had to find a way to at least try to live again for their sakes. I just couldn't go on this way.

So on a beautiful sunny day a few days later, I went into my backyard alone, sat on my old trusty wooden bench, and poured my heart out to God. I completely stripped myself bare of all emotion. I yelled and screamed at God, I questioned Him, I told Him how betrayed, angry, and lost I felt, I shook my fist at Him, I told Him how guilty I felt and then….. I begged Him to forgive me for feeling that way. I begged Him for peace in my soul, for understanding, and I begged him to help me with the anger and sadness that was overwhelming my heart. By the time I was done I felt like a wet noodle. I was completely rung out and my clothes were soaked in tears. I made a conscious decision at that very moment that even though I didn't understand why any of this had to happen, that I would trust in Him based on what I KNOW and not what I FEEL. I wasn't going to base anything off of my emotions, just on fact. Fact: Jesus loves me and died on the cross for my sins, so that I can receive eternal life. Fact: He promised to never leave me or forsake me, Deuteronomy 31:6 says "Be strong and courageous. Do not be afraid or terrified because of them, for the LORD your God goes with you ; He will never leave you nor forsake you". Fact: Even Christ himself was subjected to intense suffering, and Fact: God is compassionate, and full of grace, and he knew, and felt every single tear that I had shed over Kevin. In the Bible, 2 Samuel 12:15-23 says that David wept and prayed to God to allow his sick baby to survive. When the baby passed away 7 days later, David still worshiped the Lord and told his servants that he would see his baby again and that it would be in the presence of God. What an awesome example of faith and trust!

Only when I completely surrendered my very survival to Him did I start to feel a gradual peace slowly fall on me. I certainly couldn't have done it on my own, the anger would've eaten me alive. In Job 13:15, Job says "Though He slay me, yet will I trust Him." Job maintained his faith through all of his heartache, because he knew that it was only temporary. He knew he was going to spend eternal life in heaven, where he will never experience sadness, death, or illness again. I still have this verse on my refrigerator to this day.

That next Sunday my husband Steve suggested that we visit a church not far from our house. We didn't know a soul there, but immediately after walking in I was overcome with the most powerful, amazing feeling, and the tears just started flowing uncontrollably. The only way I know to describe how I felt is that it was similar to stepping out of a swimming pool on a cool day, cold and wet, but then the sun starts shining directly on me and begins to blanket me in total warmth. I'll never forget that feeling. I definitely was feeling God's love more than I have ever felt it before. It was like coming home, as if I had lost my way, but had finally found my way back. The Bible says in Exodus 14, "Whosoever asks, it shall be given." Well, I asked and it was given. That's not to say that I don't still have days where I feel so depressed that I can't even get out of bed, or days where I am an emotional wreck, because I definitely do. I miss my son terribly every single day, and feel as though I have lost a limb off of my own body, and now have to figure out how to function without it. Memories will creep up on me at the strangest times and hit me like an actual physical blow. I will pass by his favorite restaurant, or the park he used to play in, or the Orthodontist office where he got his braces, and just be overcome with emotion. Or I will hear a song on the radio that he loved, or a Christmas carol that we used to sing together, and just lose it. And I don't think I will ever be able to watch American Idol again. The only difference now is that I know I am not dealing with anything alone, I never was. Psalm 46:10 says "Be still and know that I am God," so I have to pray about it, be still, and let God quiet the storm inside of me. I have to remember that He can't do that if I am always standing in the way though. A deacon at my church once said "When you are in a hole, quit digging!" And, boy is he right! I just had to get out of God's way. You can't tell God something that He doesn't already know, so I believe He was just waiting for me to surrender and confess my heart and my feelings completely to Him. I made myself 100% vulnerable to Him that day. God already knew about my anger, depression, and utter desperation, He just wanted me to put my trust in Him and Him alone. I couldn't depend on people to rescue me, only my savior. The late and great Billy Graham said "When we come to the end of ourselves, we come to the beginning of God." I think it's safe to say that I had definitely hit the end of the road trying to do things on my own, so there was nowhere else for me to look, but up.

I read a Christian article somewhere that said when you are doubting God's love, to sit down and try to think of all of the blessings that you received during your difficult time in order to realize that God, in fact, was there with you the entire time. I did this, and they were right. God truly had blessed me in so many ways, but I was just too stubborn and blind to realize it at the time. Here is just a few of those blessings:

-Two days before my mom passed away, she became very alert, sat up straight in her bed, looked over at Slade and me and said, " You are going to think I'm crazy but there is an angel right by my head and I can feel the wind from its wings." We were stunned and amazed, so I pressed her for more detail and she told me that the angel was beautiful and that the wings were not made of feathers, but of hair. What an incredible image! I know that God sent that angel to comfort my mom, calm her fears, and to escort her to her new heavenly home.

-About a week before Kevin passed away, my son Slade brought home a brown bulldog (a pitbull to be exact) with a body full of muscle, huge radar ears, and strong powerful jaws that needed a home. I was very unhappy about this and did not want a "vicious" dog in our house trying to maul us. Well, after a lot of persuasion and begging my husband and I agreed to temporarily (yeah right) let him stay. Little did I know that this dog would make such a huge impact on our family. I spent most of my time in my backyard in the weeks following Kevin's death because I just couldn't stand being closed up inside the house. This dog that I didn't want , with his huge teeth, and intimidating stare, refused to leave my side. He would crawl into my lap on the bench and let me hug him and cry into his fur. No matter how long it took, he would not move until I would quit crying. He would look deeply into my eyes as if he understood that I needed to be comforted, and gently lick the tears off of my face. Needless to say, I was a gonner for sure. I fell in love with this dog, and decided he was never leaving us! There is never a day that goes by that he doesn't make us laugh with his goofy personality. And trust me, we sure could use a little laughter in our lives. He has been like a little ray of sweet sunshine to us in some very difficult times. I don't even mind that he loves my son the most! Call me crazy, but

I truly believe that God put this dog in our lives at that particular time, for that reason.

-The first time we visited our church, I noticed while reading the bulletin that they offered a grief class. My husband urged me to sign up and offered to go with me. We went a few nights later and I was a complete bundle of nerves and on the verge of a very large panic attack. The thought of opening up my heart to complete strangers made me feel sick to my stomach. After just a few minutes though, I began to realize that these people were full of Christ's love and were hurting as much as I was. I have never met such sweet, caring, and down to earth people in my whole life! They physically and emotionally embraced me from the very first moment that we met. They would call to check up on me and quickly made us a part of their family, and I will forever be grateful to them for their love, support, and gentle ministering. They saw me at my absolute worst, and yet they still loved and accepted me. Their actions reminded me that God loved me through it all. He loved me at my best, and at my worst. He even loved me when most people would say that I was unlovable.

-Remember when I prayed for Kevin to smile again? One morning a couple of months after we lost him, Slade ran into the kitchen with tears running down his face and said that he had a dream about his brother. He said that Kevin was looking at him and smiling from ear to ear, he then looked down at a cross necklace that was around his neck and showed it to Slade. He smiled again and then he disappeared. Slade recognized the necklace because It was the same diamond cross necklace that he had bought me for my birthday the year before, and I wear it every single day. In my heart I know that the dream was God's way of assuring us that Kevin is now smiling with his Saviour in heaven. Praise Jesus! My God is such an awesome God! He heard my prayer and my son smiled again! Maybe not here on Earth, but surely in heaven. That was just another example of God's endless love and compassion.

-One week after Kevin passed away, I received a box with some of his personal belongings from his apartment. At the very top of that box laid his Bible, and the pages in it were very worn. What a blessing it is to know that my son was still reading his Bible!

-God has put some amazing people in my life. My very good friend who lived in Ohio at the time, moved here to South Carolina recently and bought a house 2 miles from mine. What a blessing! She has supported me and hugged me through my tears more times than I could ever count. She is one of the most generous and compassionate people I know. She constantly makes me laugh and never lets me get swallowed up in self pity. She even made me a beautiful memorial garden in my backyard with colorful flowers, solar lights, and even a hand painted Tweety Bird rock! She worked so hard on that garden to make it special, and It was one of the most thoughtful things anyone has ever done for me. Another friend of mine, whom I had lost touch with over the years due to us moving out of state, just popped up out of nowhere one day after not seeing her for 10 years. I bumped into her at a store recently and we have picked up right where we left off. She is full of Christian wisdom and strength and has been such an emotional support to me. It's as if she just showed up when I needed her most. Definitely a God thing! They have both been through some trying times themselves, but are always there to help others, including me. What wonderful ladies! They inspire me to try to be a better person.

So you see, God was there all along. I was just too consumed in my pain to see it.

I am still a work in progress, I think we all are. I still sleep with my cell phone by my head expecting Kevin's call, and jump every time it rings. I feel a sense of panic every time my husband or son leaves the house, and jump out of my skin when I hear sirens. And I will probably always feel like I am on the outside looking in, but I will have to remember that Isaiah 41:10 says "So do not fear, for I am with you; do not be dismayed, for I am your God. I will strengthen you and help you; I will uphold you with my righteous right hand."

I just have to be honest with myself, I am a very different person now, but with my Father's help I have learned to accept that. I had to mourn my old self and now I am asking God to mold me into the person He has always wanted me to be. So instead of running AWAY from God, I'm running TO God, just as fast as I can. Now when the Devil whispers in my ear (which he does quite often)

"This world would be a better place without you in it" or "You are worthless and impossible to love", I remind him that I am a child of God, highly favored, and created for a purpose. I am loved unconditionally by the Creator, and was born because He chose it to be so. Also, If I'm having an especially tough day, I will go outside, lay on my lounge chair with the dog that I didn't want, put my headphones on, and blast Christian music into my ears to let the promises of God's love and forgiveness soak in. And then I thank Him for all of the times that He has blessed me, and for refusing to give up on me.

I don't worry about not fitting in anymore, because as long as I belong to God, I don't need to fit in. And now when I walk by our "Thank you Jesus" sign, I smile, and remember how He rescued me from the deepest depths of depression and despair. I look up and thank Him for loving a sinner like me, and for always keeping His promises, even when I doubted Him.

So, If you ever find yourself doubting your faith, or struggling with heavy burdens, please don't lose hope, and just remember to keep your eyes on Jesus. Call out to the Saviour for help and "be still" while He works in your life. Just give it all to the one who created it all, and remember that you truly are never alone. God's perfect love is infinite and never ending, and He will never break His promises to you.

Now when people ask me how I can trust in God after all that has happened, I simply reply: How could I not?

Acknowledgments

I would first like to thank my heavenly Father for His unconditional love and forgiveness. I also would like to thank my husband Steve for your unending strength and support, and for letting me constantly bounce ideas off of you. I love you endlessly. I am proud to be your wife. To my son, Slade who even through your own sadness and grief, was always more worried about me than yourself. You have a heart of gold and I love who you are. I'm proud to be your mom. To my sweet friend Kim, thank you for your endless love and support, and most of all for your friendship. You have always been there for me, and for that I will be forever grateful. To my friends Debbie and Billy, thank you for your Godly wisdom and encouragement, without it, I'm not sure I would have written my story. And to Socastee Baptist Church, thank you for being a church that is so full of love and compassion, and for always standing solid on the word of God.

Kevin's death has to have a purpose. If I have helped just one person with his story, then it will not have been in vain. May God Bless you all.

In loving memory of

My son, Kevin.

Until we meet again

You Are Always There For Me

When the world comes crashing in

And chaos rules my mind,

I turn my heart to you, Lord,

And pure, sweet peace I find.

You lift me out of trouble

You comfort me in pain,

You nourish, heal and cleanse me,

Like cool, refreshing rain.

In times of joy and bliss,

When things are going right,

You lift me even higher,

And fill me with delight.

You listen to my prayers;

You hear my every plea;

I'm safe because I know

You're always there for me.

By Joanna Fuchs

About Carfentanil

Carfentanil is a more powerful and dangerous derivative of Fentanil. It is one of the most potent opioids known. It is 10,000 times more potent than Morphine, and 4,000 times more potent than Heroin. This drug is most commonly known to be used as an anesthetic for elephants. It is so dangerous that veterinarians have to use protective gear when handling it so that they don't breathe it in or absorb it through their skin.

A dose the size of a single grain of salt is enough to cause overdose and death in a human being. A scary fact is, that starting in July of 2016, Carfentanil was found in Heroin and other drugs that were being sold on the streets. It is often added to these drugs without the buyers' knowledge because it looks like any other drug, and has no odor and has the consistency of a white powder. Sadly, more than 142 Americans die every single day from drug overdoses, and 60% of them involve Opioids.

Addiction Hotline- 1-800-815-6308

THE WHITE HOUSE

WASHINGTON

May 25, 2018

Ms. Kim MacDowell
Myrtle Beach, South Carolina

Dear Ms. MacDowell,

Thank you for sharing your story with me. I am so terribly sorry to hear of the loss of your son, Kevin. Melania and I send our prayers to you and your family.

Opioid abuse is a national health emergency. Too many of our fellow Americans have been lost due to the scourge of drug abuse. It is plaguing families and communities across our Nation, robbing so many of their potential. My Administration is fighting this crisis on all fronts, and examples like yours motivate me to keep up the fight.

I want the next generation of young Americans to know the blessings of a drug-free life. As a Nation, we remember those we have lost, lift up those struggling with addiction, and pray for every family member or friend who has been touched by this awful disaster. Together, we will face this challenge as a national family with conviction, with unity, and with commitment to love and support our neighbors in times of dire need. We will overcome addiction in America.

Thank you again for taking the time to write. The prayers of our Nation are with you and your family.

Sincerely,

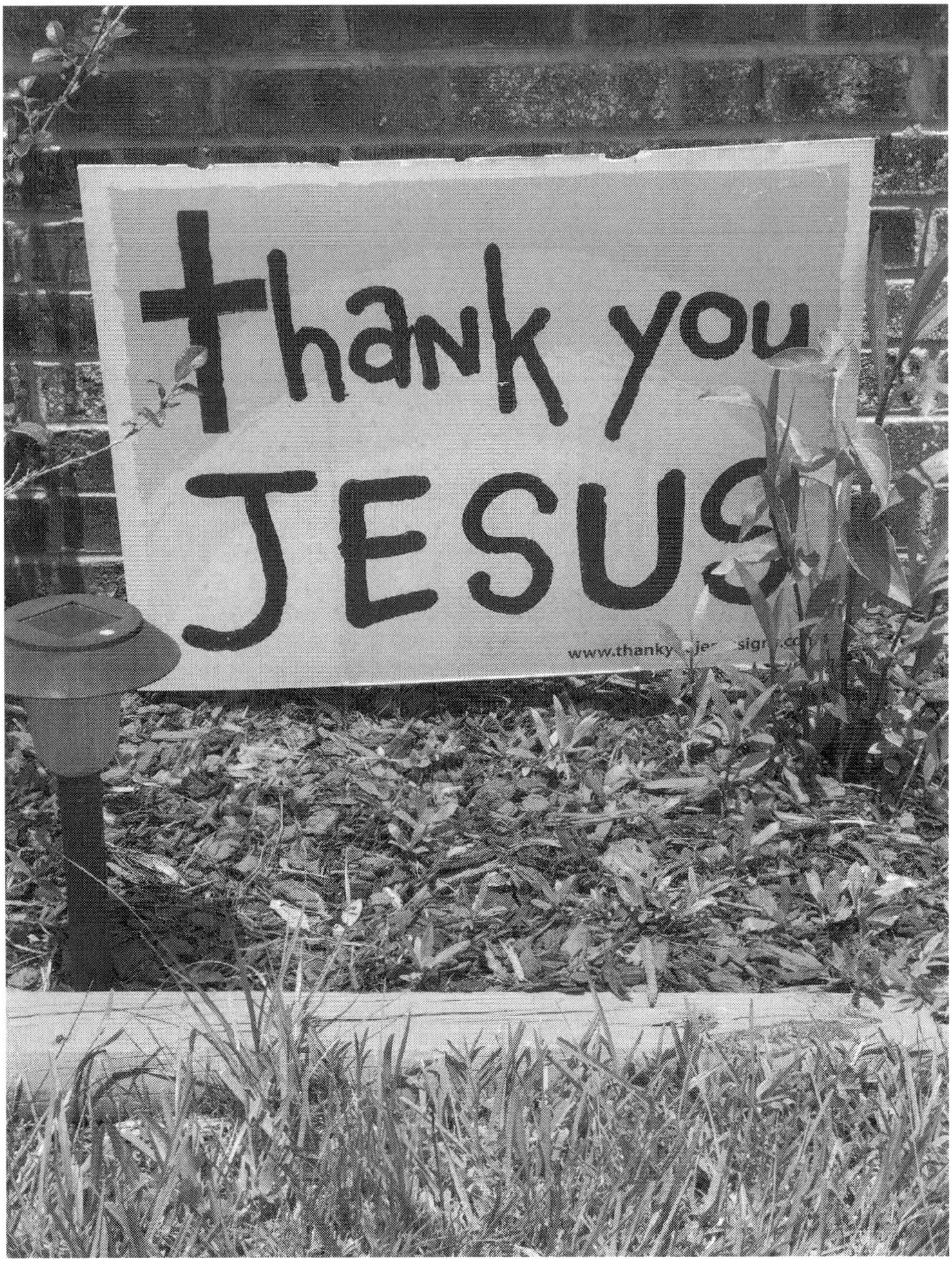
thank you
JESUS

Made in the USA
Columbia, SC
30 August 2018